OUT OF THIS WORLD TRUTHS ABOUT THE SOLAR SYSTEM ASTRONOMY 5TH GRADE

ASTRONOMY & SPACE SCIENCE

BABY PROFESSOR

EDUCATION KIDS

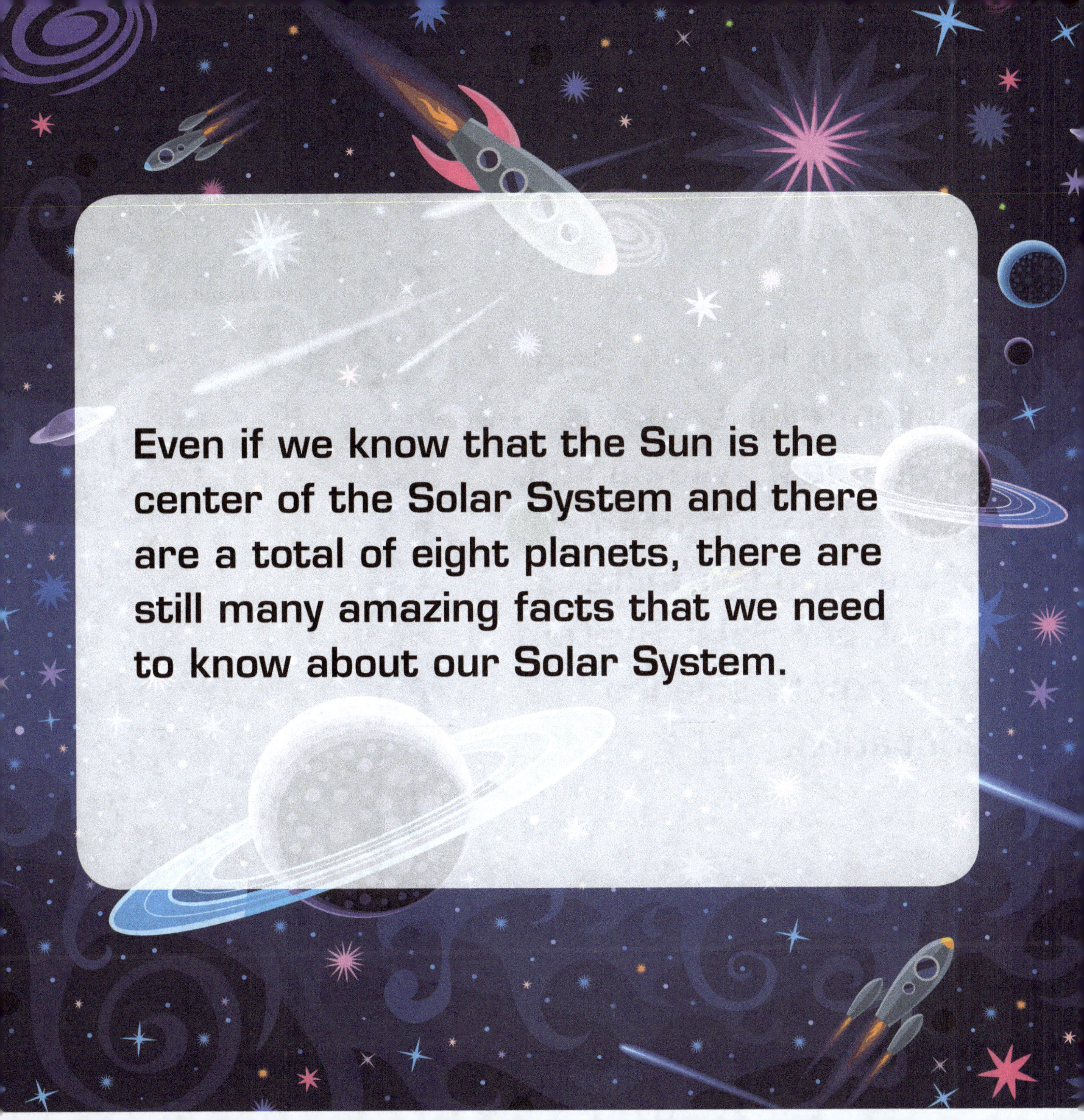

Even if we know that the Sun is the center of the Solar System and there are a total of eight planets, there are still many amazing facts that we need to know about our Solar System.

Exploring how our Solar System evolved is the key to our past. We cannot ignore the importance of knowing the facts about our Solar System to promote science education.

Jupiter
rth
Mars
Uranus
Saturn
Neptune

LET'S BEGIN LEARNING
MORE INFORMATION
ABOUT OUR SOLAR
SYSTEM AND THE GALAXY
IT IS PART OF

MILKY WAY

Our Solar System is out at one edge of the Milky Way galaxy. The center of the Milky Way has a very huge black hole known as Sagittarius A, with a mass of about 4.3 million suns.

Our home galaxy will collide with its neighbor galaxy, Andromeda, in around 4 billion years.

The collision will not be a problem for us on Earth, because by that far in the future, our Solar System will have changed. Our Sun will become a red giant before then, and life on Earth would no longer be possible.

PLANET NINE

The mass of the ninth planet could be about 10 times of Earth's mass and 5,000 times of Pluto. It is also known as **Planet X**

The evidence of the ninth planet's existence was revealed on January 20, 2016. Nobody has found this planet yet, but scientists are searching. It orbits around the Sun 20 times farther than Neptune.

DWARF PLANETS

Ceres, Pluto, Eris, Haumea, and Makemake are the first five recognized dwarf planets. Just like other planets, they orbit around the Sun along with asteroids and comets.

Ceres was discovered by Giuseppe Piazzi as the first and largest asteroid in the Solar System on January 1, 1801.

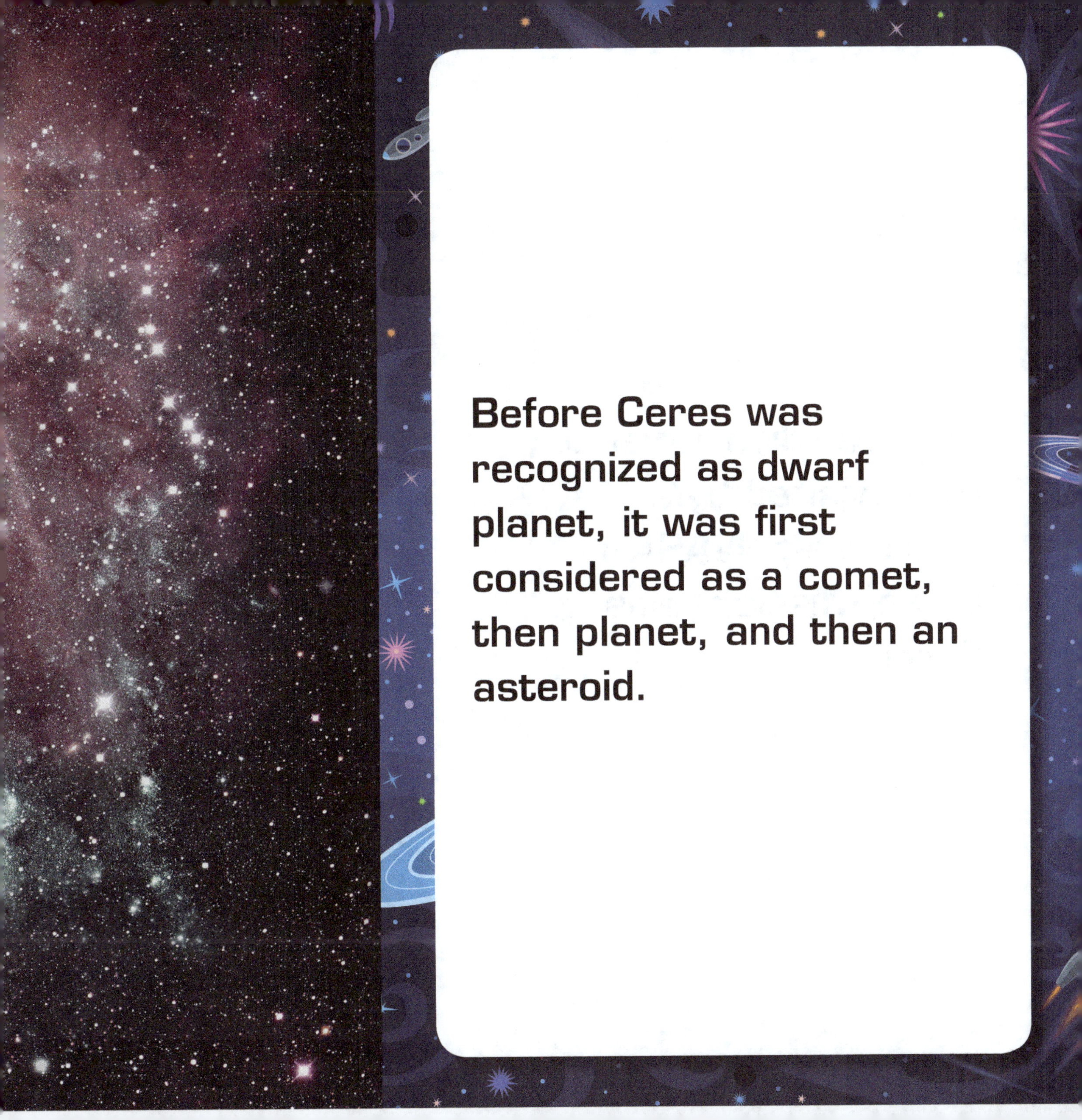

Before Ceres was recognized as dwarf planet, it was first considered as a comet, then planet, and then an asteroid.

The first dwarf planet
to be visited by a
spacecraft, NASA's
Dawn Mission, was
Ceres.

METEORS AND METEORITES

It is estimated by scientists that 44,000 kilograms or about 48.5 tons of meteoritic materials fall on Earth every day.

This is what we call meteor showers. The most famous meteor shower is the Perseids, which streak across the sky every year, around August 12.

VENUS TRANSIT

A Transit of Venus is when Venus passes between the Earth and the Sun. This last happened in June, 2012.

The orbit of Venus is a
little tilted compared
to Earth's, so most
of the time Venus
passes higher or lower
between us and the
Sun. The next time it
will occur would be in
2117.

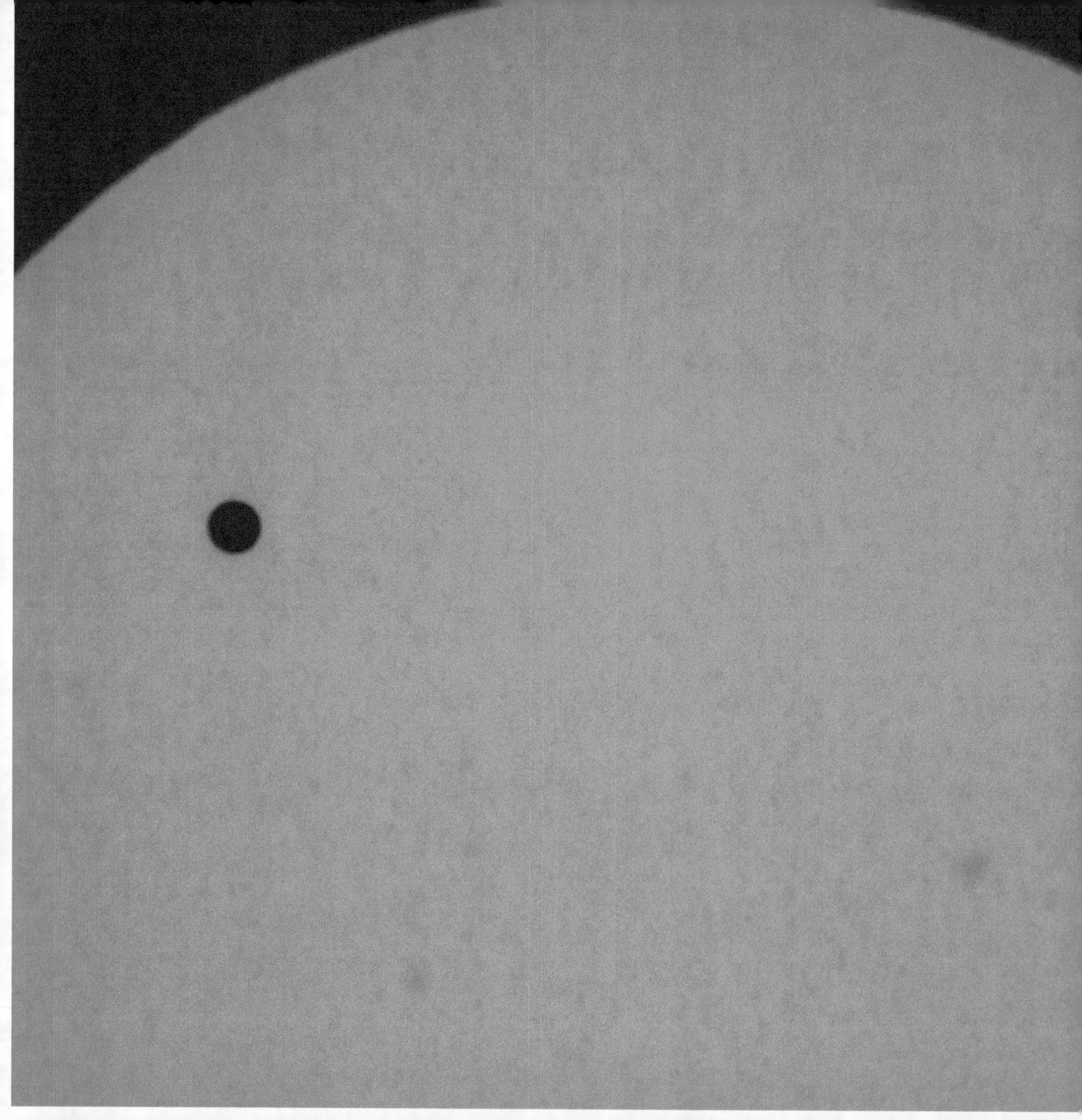

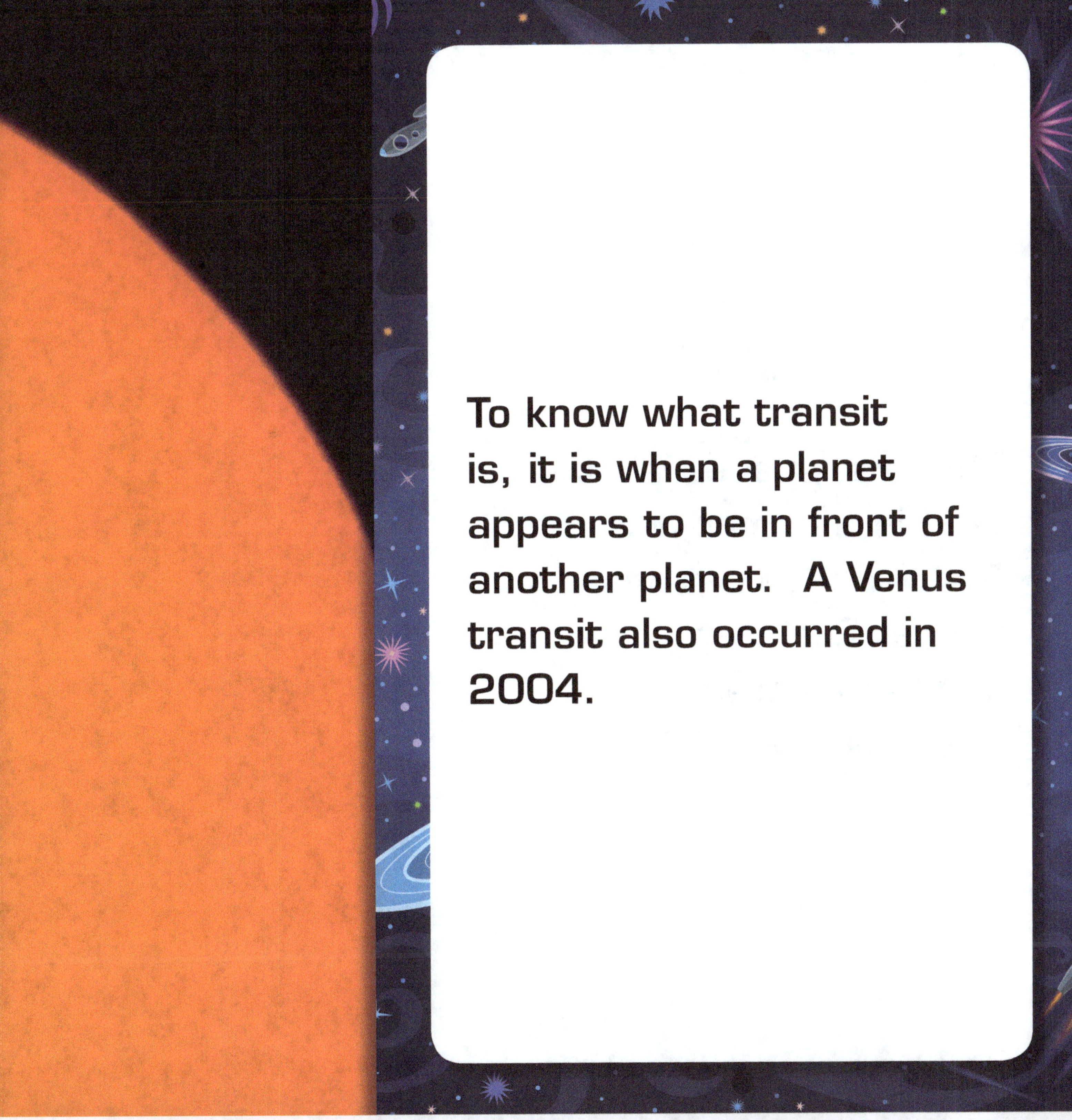

To know what transit
is, it is when a planet
appears to be in front of
another planet. A Venus
transit also occurred in
2004.

COMET

The first spacecraft to land in a comet was NASA's International Comet Explorer. The comet was Giacobini-Zinner.

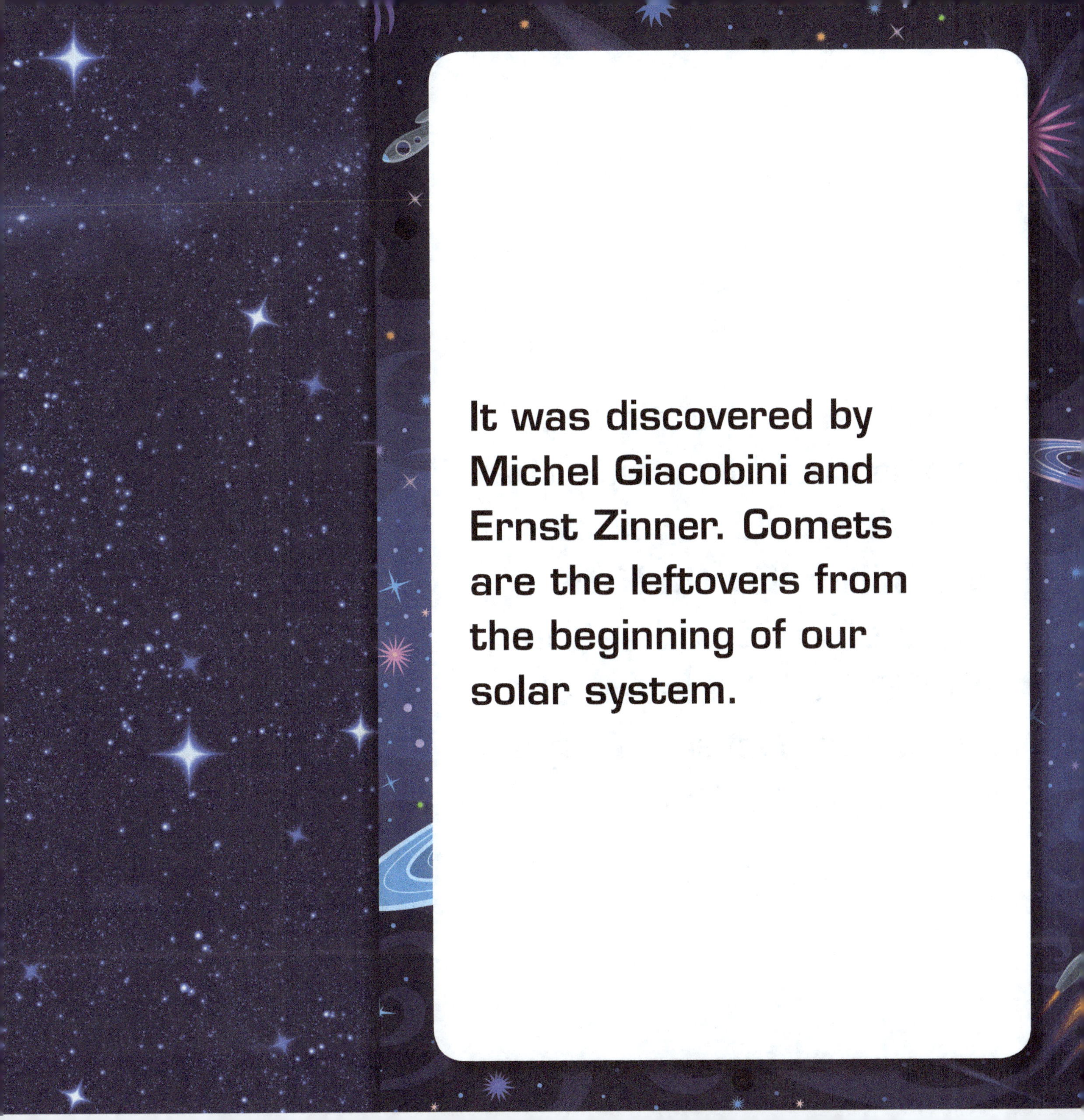

It was discovered by Michel Giacobini and Ernst Zinner. Comets are the leftovers from the beginning of our solar system.

SUN

Do you know how many Earths could fit inside the Sun? It would cover over one million Earths! The mass of the Sun is about 99.86% of the mass of our Solar System. That's how huge the Sun is!

How hot is the Sun? Its temperature reaches up to 15 million °C at its core. If a planet or any celestial object goes near it, it would be totally wiped out.

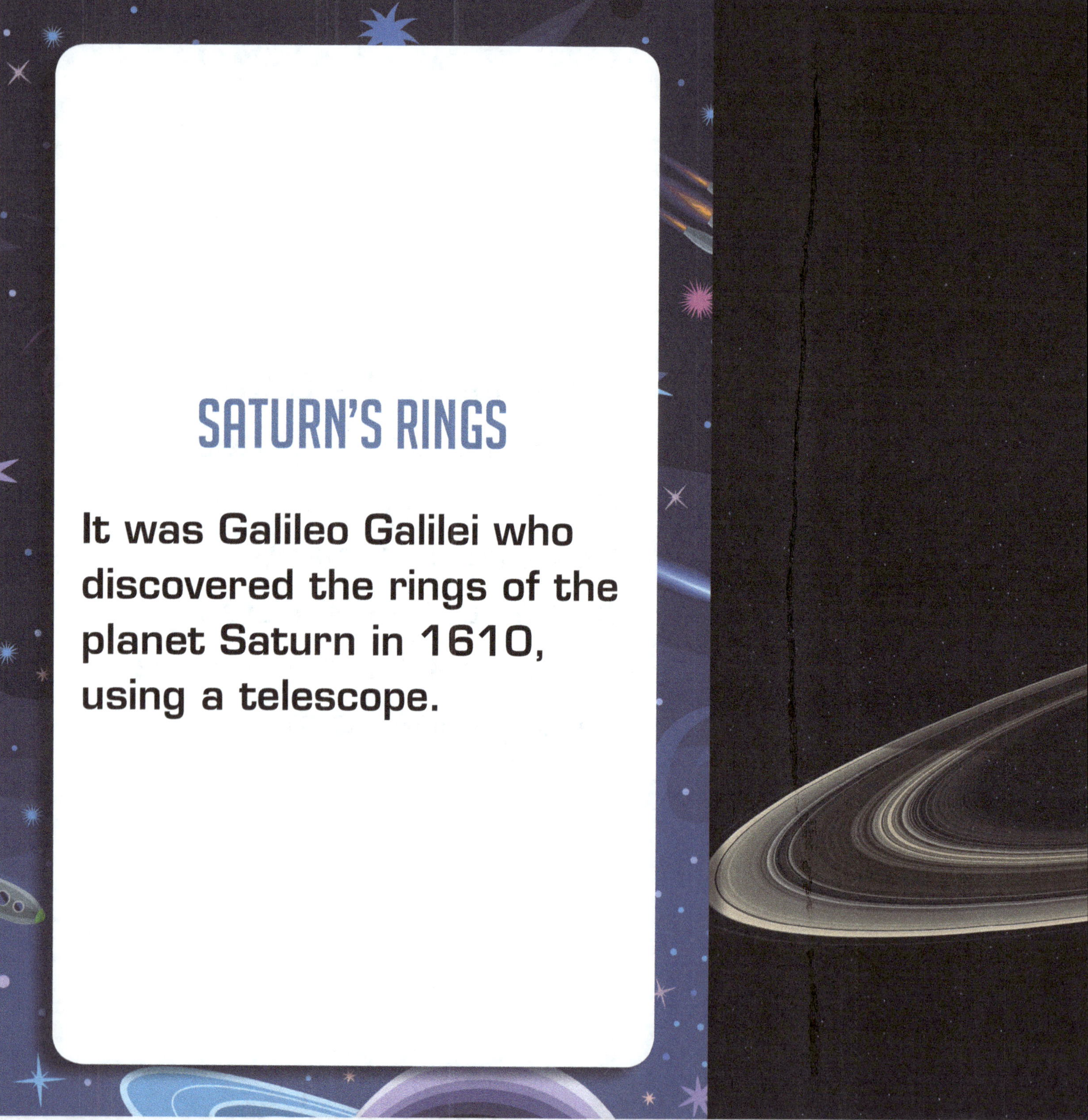

SATURN'S RINGS

It was Galileo Galilei who discovered the rings of the planet Saturn in 1610, using a telescope.

Jupiter
Earth
Venus
Mars
Saturn

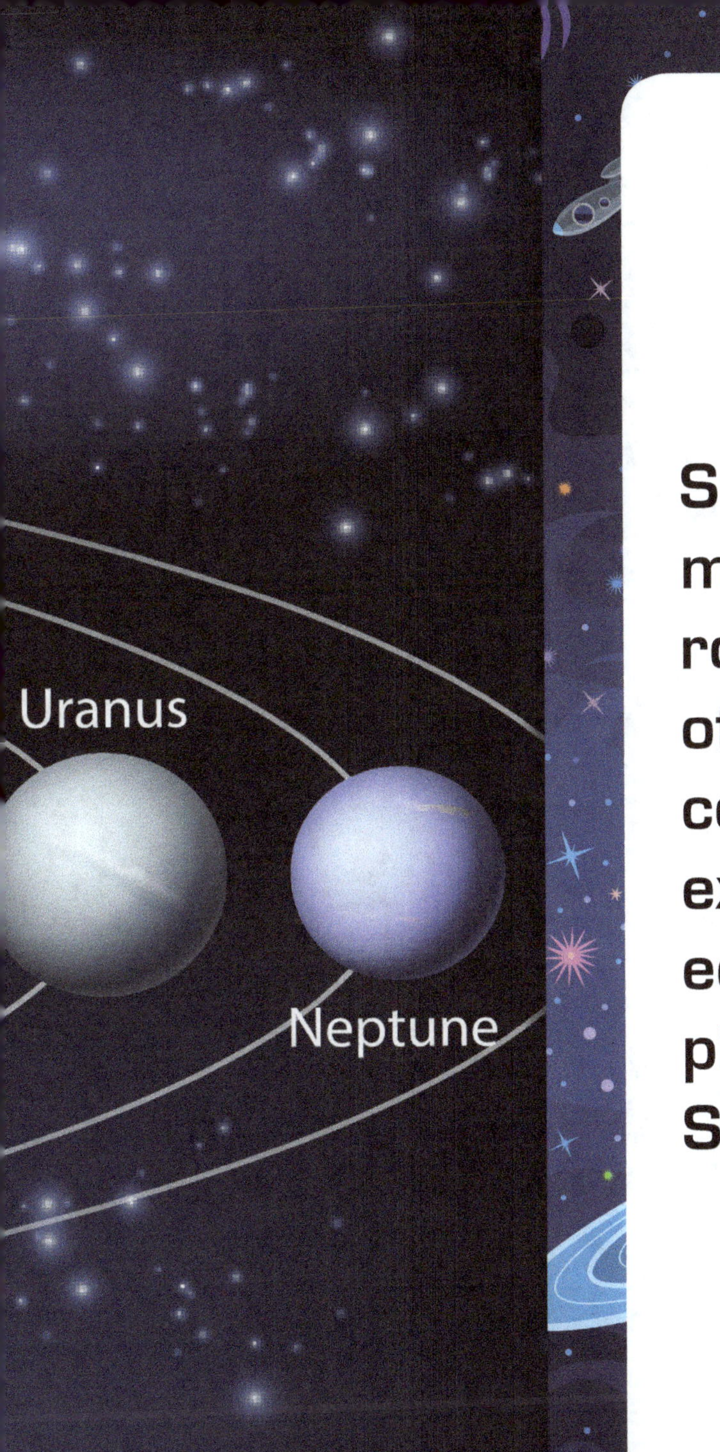

Saturn has 7 rings made up of dust, ice, rocks, and even remains of asteroids and comets. The planet's extensive rings have no equal around the other planets in the Solar System.

Four spacecraft have
visited Saturn: Voyager
1 and 2, Pioneer 11,
and Cassini-Huygens.
The spacecraft that
continues gathering
data about the planet,
its rings, and moons is
the Cassini-Huygens.
It's mission will end in
September, 2017, when
it crashes into Saturn.

MOON

Every year the moon moves about 3.8 centimeters further away from Earth. The current orbit of the moon around the Earth takes 27.3 days and since the moon is estimated to continue moving away from our planet for about 50 billion years, at the end of that time it will take 47 days for the moon to orbit around the Earth.

BLACK HOLES

Do you know that there are famous black holes in our Solar System? These black holes are Cygnus X-1, Sagittarius A*, M87, and Centaurus A.

Cygnus X-1 is 14.8 times the mass of the Sun and it's about 6,070 light years away from Earth. Sagittarius A* can be found at the center of our home galaxy, the Milky Way, and its mass is about the mass of about 4 million Suns.

There is a massive black
hole at the center of M87
or Messier 87 galaxy
which has a mass of about
3.5 billion Suns. The black
hole that can be found in
the center of Centaurus
A galaxy is about 55
million times the mass of
the Sun.

Io

This moon has a surface temperature of -163 °C and was discovered by Galileo Galilei on January 8, 1610. Unlike Earth's moon, which is inactive, Io's surface has more than 400 active volcanoes, making it the solar system's most active volcanic world.

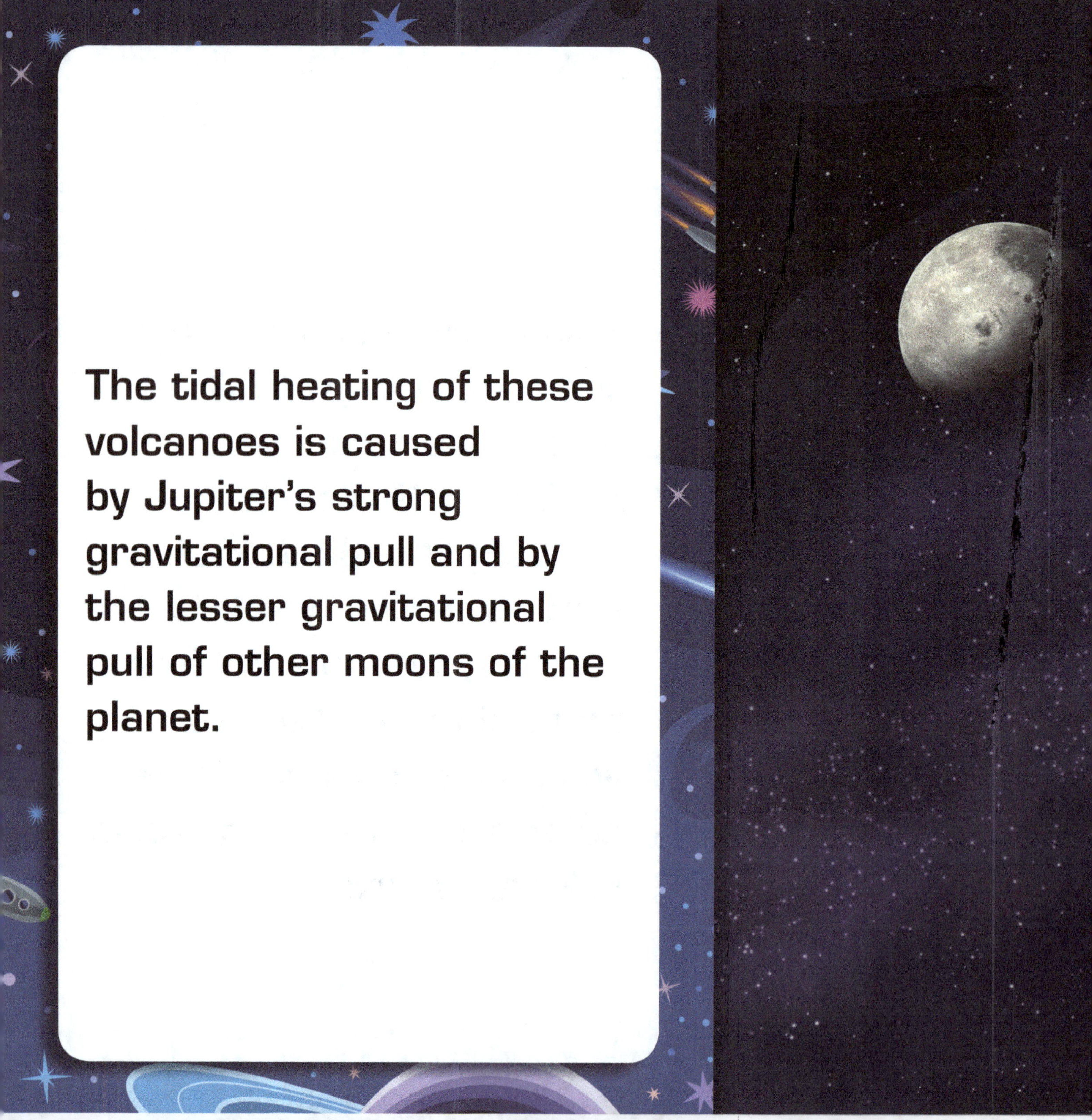

The tidal heating of these volcanoes is caused by Jupiter's strong gravitational pull and by the lesser gravitational pull of other moons of the planet.

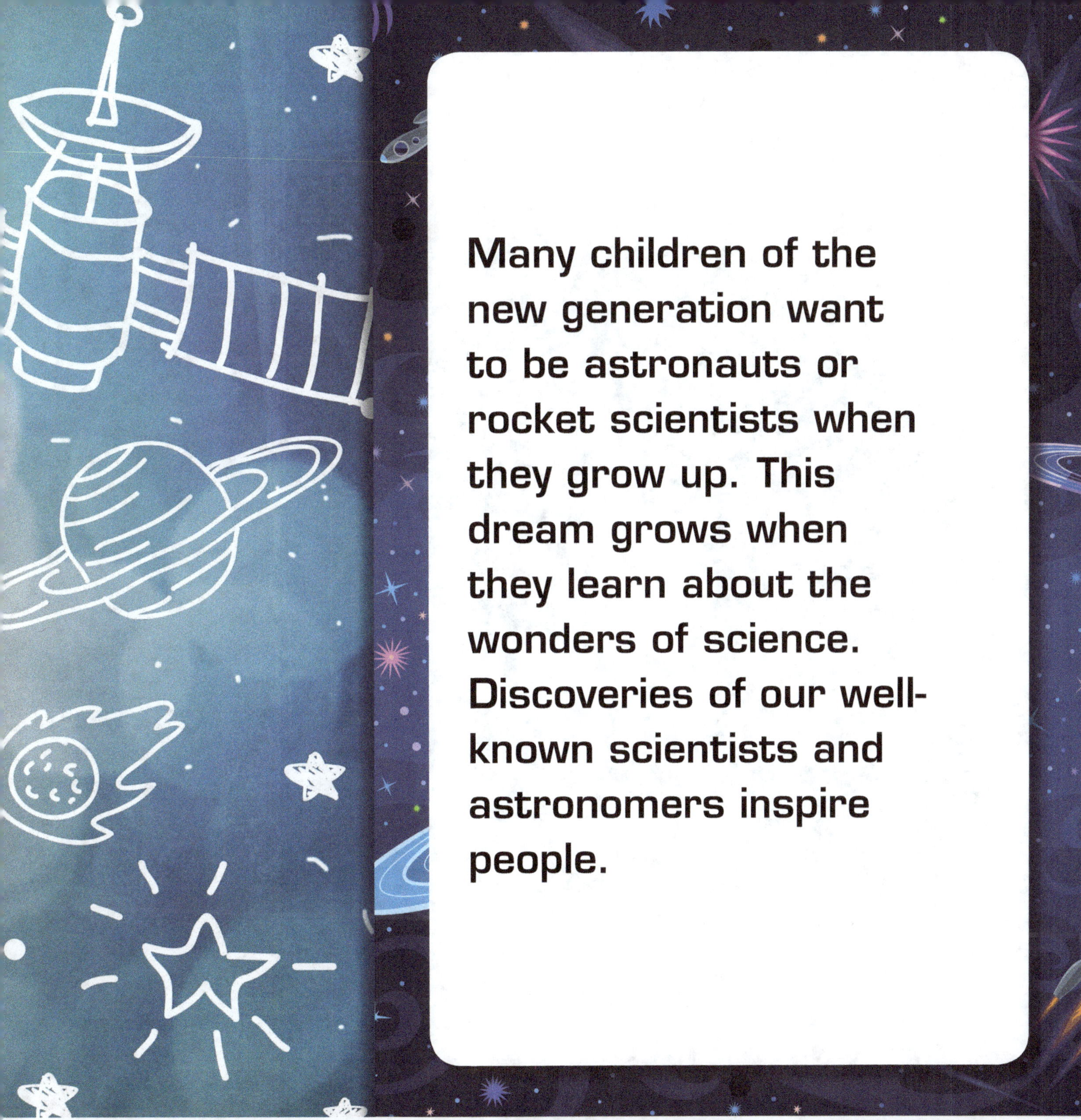

Many children of the new generation want to be astronauts or rocket scientists when they grow up. This dream grows when they learn about the wonders of science. Discoveries of our well-known scientists and astronomers inspire people.

Visit

BABY PROFESSOR
EDUCATION KIDS

www.BabyProfessorBooks.com

to download Free Baby Professor eBooks
and view our catalog of new and exciting
Children's Books